1. Parengarenga Harbour
2. Great Barrier Island
3. Tiritiri Matangi Island
4. Miranda Shorebird Center
5. Rotoura Lakes & Mokoia Island
6. Pureora Forest Park
7. Manawatu Estuary
8. Ahuriri Estuary
9. Mount Bruce Wildlife Center
10. Kapiti Island Nature Reserve
11. Farewell Spit
12. Kahurangi National Park
13. Otago Peninsula
14. Arthur's Pass National Park
15. Mount Aspiring National Park
16. Okarito Lagoon
17. Kaki Visitor Hide
18. Milford Track – Fiordland
19. Stewart Island
20. Chatham Island

TASMAN SEA
NORTH ISLAND
Auckland
SOUTH PACIFIC OCEAN
Wellington
Christchurch
SOUTH ISLAND
Dunedin

978-1-58355-889-8
$7.95 U.S.
$9.95 CAN
50795
9 781583 558898

8 84682 01066 9

T0123923

NEW ZEALAND BIRDS

A Folding Pocket Guide to Familiar Species

NEW ZEALAND BIRDS – A Folding Pocket Guide to Familiar Species

WATERFORD PRESS

Made in the USA

KIWIS

Brown Kiwi
Apteryx australis To 40 cm (16 in.)
Flightless, cone-shaped birds live in burrows and are most active at night. The most common and widespread species of New Zealand's national bird.

Great Spotted Kiwi
Apteryx haastii
To 45 cm (18 in.)
Note barred plumage. The similar-looking little spotted kiwi (*A. owenii*) is 30 cm (12 in.) in length.

WATERBIRDS & NEARSHORE BIRDS

New Zealand Dabchick
Poliocephalus rufopectus
To 30 cm (12 in.)

Great Crested Grebe
Podiceps cristatus To 50 cm (20 in.)

Grey Duck
Anas superciliosa To 60 cm (2 ft.)
Striped face is distinctive. Also called parera.

Mallard
Anas platyrhynchos To 70 cm. (28 in.)

Paradise Shelduck
Tadorna variegata To 65 cm (26 in.)
Common throughout New Zealand.

New Zealand Scaup
Aythya novaeseelandiae
To 40 cm (16 in.)
Plumage is glossy. New Zealand's only diving duck; a protected endemic.

Australasian Shoveler
Anas rhynchotis To 55 cm (22 in.)
Large bill is wedge-shaped.

Grey Teal
Anas gracilis To 50 cm (20 in.)
Note red eye and blue-grey bill.

WATERBIRDS & NEARSHORE BIRDS

Pied Shag
Phalacrocorax varius
To 83 cm (33 in.)
Note yellow patch in front of eye.

Black Shag
Phalacrocorax carbo
To 85 cm (34 in.)
Note yellow throat patch.

Little Black Shag
Phalacrocorax sulcirostris
To 70 cm (28 in.)
Similar, but smaller than the black shag. More common on North Island.

Little Shag
Phalacrocorax melanoleucos
To 60 cm (2 ft.)
Stocky shag has a stubby, yellow bill.

Rockhopper Penguin
Eudyptes chrysocome
To 60 cm (2 ft.)
Small penguin has yellow head plumes that are not joined across the forehead.

Spotted Shag
Stictocarbo punctatus
To 75 cm (30 in.)
Note bluish face and two head crests.

Blue Penguin
Eudyptula minor
To 40 cm (16 in.)
Also known as fairy penguin and little penguin, it is found on coastlines throughout New Zealand.

Yellow-eyed Penguin
Megadyptes antipodes
To 65 cm (26 in.)
The only penguin with yellow eyes.

Erect-crested Penguin
Eudyptes sclateri
To 70 cm (28 in.)
Eye plumes sweep upward.

Black Swan
Cygnus atratus
To 1.4 m (56 in.)

Feral Goose
Anser anser
To 83 cm (33 in.)
Note thick neck.

Canada Goose
Branta canadensis
To 1.1 m (45 in.)

WATERBIRDS & NEARSHORE BIRDS

Royal Spoonbill
Platalea regia
To 75 cm (30 in.)
Bill has a spoon-shaped tip.

Cattle Egret
Bubulcus ibis coromandus
To 50 cm (20 in.)

White-faced Heron
Ardea novaehollandiae
To 65 cm (26 in.)

Australasian Bittern
Botaurus poiciloptilus
To 75 cm (30 in.)
Wetland bird.

White Heron
Ardea alba
To 95 cm (38 in.)
Note yellow bill and black feet.

Reef Heron
Egretta sacra
To 65 cm (26 in.)
Slate-grey heron is the one most likely seen on ocean shores.

Eurasian Coot
Fulica atra
To 40 cm (16 in.)

Pukeko
Porphyrio porphyrio
To 50 cm (20 in.)
Wetland bird.

Spotless Crake
Porzana tabuensis
To 20 cm (8 in.)
Wetland bird.

Banded Rail
Rallus philippensis
To 33 cm (13 in.)
Marsh bird has distinctive call that sounds like a rusty gate.

Weka
Gallirallus australis
To 53 cm (21 in.)
Flightless brown to greyish bird inhabits shrubby areas.

Marsh Crake
Porzana pusilla
To 18 cm (7 in.)
Note barred flanks.

WATERBIRDS & NEARSHORE BIRDS

South Island Pied Oystercatcher
Haematopus finschi
To 48 cm (19 in.)

Variable Oystercatcher
Haematopus unicolor
To 48 cm (19 in.)

Bar-tailed Godwit
Limosa lapponica
To 50 cm (20 in.)
Long bill is slightly upturned. Non-breeding plumage is greyish.

New Zealand Dotterel
Charadrius obscurus
To 28 cm (11 in.)

Pacific Golden Plover
Pluvialis fulva
To 28 cm (11 in.)

Ruddy Turnstone
Arenaria interpres
To 25 cm (10 in.)

Banded Dotterel
Charadrius bicinctus
To 20 cm (8 in.)

Pied Stilt
Himantopus leucocephalus
To 40 cm (16 in.)

Black Stilt
Himantopus novaezelandiae
To 40 cm (16 in.)
Endemic species is critically endangered.

Spotless Dotterel

Wrybill
Anarhynchus frontalis
To 20 cm (8 in.)
Endemic species.

Lesser Knot
Calidris canutus
To 30 cm (12 in.)
Plump, red-breasted shorebird is an abundant migrant.

Masked Lapwing
Vanellus miles
To 38 cm (15 in.)
Also called spur-winged plover.

White-fronted Tern
Sterna striata
To 43 cm (17 in.)
Note black bill and feet.
New Zealand's most
common tern.

Black-fronted Tern
Childonias albostriatus
To 30 cm (12 in.)
Note yellow-orange
bill and feet.

Red-billed Gull
Chroicocephalus scopulinus
To 38 cm (15 in.)

Caspian Tern
Hydroprogne caspia
To 60 cm (2 ft.)
Note large
size and stout
orange bill.

Black-billed Gull
Larus bulleri
To 38 cm (15 in.)

Southern Black-backed Gull
Larus dominicanus
To 58 cm (23 in.)
Note large size
and all-white tail.

Sooty Shearwater
Puffinus griseus
To 45 cm (18 in.)
Dark bird has
distinctive shearing
flight pattern, dipping
from side to side as it
glides stiff-winged.

Australasian Gannet
Morus serrator
To 1 m (40 in.)
Large white seabird
has black wing tips.

New Zealand Kingfisher
Halcyon sancta vagans
To 25 cm (10 in.)

Grey-faced Petrel
Pterodroma macroptera
To 40 cm (16 in.)
Dark seabird has
a grey face.

Southern Skua
Stercorarius antarctica
To 65 cm (26 in.)
Large brown seabird
is common on
outlying islands.

Royal Albatross
Diomedea epomophora
To 1.2 m (4 ft.)
Has pale pink bill and feet
and a clean, black and
white appearance.

New Zealand Falcon
Falco novaeseelandiae
To 48 cm (19 in.)

Australasian Harrier
Circus approximans
To 60 cm (2 ft.)
Hunts in open
lowlands where it
glides very slowly
close to the ground
while scanning
for prey.

Morepork
Ninox novaeseelandiae
To 35 cm (14 in.)
Name-saying
call – more-pork –
is a common
nighttime sound.

Spotted Dove
Streptopelia chinensis tigrina
To 30 cm (12 in.)

New Zealand Pigeon
Hemiphaga novaeseelandiae
To 50 cm (20 in.)

Little Owl
Athene noctua
To 25 cm (10 in.)
Call is a sharp –
KEE-ew.

Rock Dove
Columba livia
To 35 cm (14 in.)

Barbary Dove
Streptopelia roseogrisea
To 28 cm (11 in.)

Chukor
Alectoris chukar
To 35 cm (14 in.)

Wild Turkey
Meleagris gallopavo
To 1.2 m (4 ft.)

California Quail
Callipepla californica
To 25 cm (10 in.)

Ring-necked Pheasant
Phasianus colchicus
To 90 cm (3 ft.)

Common Peafowl
Pavo cristatus
To 2 m (80 in.)

Kea
Nestor notabilis
To 45 cm (18 in.)
Olive green parrot has
reddish underwings.
Locally common on
South Island.

Yellow-crowned Parakeet
Cyanoramphus auriceps
To 25 cm (10 in.)

Red-crowned Parakeet
Cyanoramphus novaezelandiae
To 28 cm (11 in.)

Kaka
Nestor meridionalis
To 45 cm (18 in.)
Plumage color varies.
Distinguished from
the similar kea by its
silvery cap.

Kakapo
Strigops habroptilus
To 63 cm (25 in.)
Endemic species is
the largest parrot in
the world and the
only flightless parrot.
Critically endangered.

Sulphur-crested Cockatoo
Cacatua galerita
To 35 cm (14 in.)

Crimson Rosella
Platycercus elegans
To 40 cm (16 in.)

Eastern Rosella
Platycercus eximius
To 33 cm (13 in.)

Shining Cuckoo
Chrysococcyx lucidus
To 20 cm (8 in.)
Green plumage is
metallic. Like other
cuckoos, it is a
brood parasite and
lays its eggs in the
nests of other birds.

Fairy Martin
Hirundo ariel
To 13 cm (5 in.)

Long-tailed Cuckoo
Eudynamys taitensis
To 40 cm (16 in.)

Welcome Swallow
Hirundo neoxena
To 15 cm (6 in.)

Rifleman
Acanthisitta chloris
To 8 cm (3 in.)
New Zealand's
smallest bird.

Rock Wren
Xenicus gilviventris
To 10 cm (4 in.)
Small alpine bird
has a very short tail.

Skylark
Alauda arvensis
To 18 cm (7 in.)
Stocky, brown
bird with streaked
plumage.

Yellowhead
Mohoua ochrocephala
To 15 cm (6 in.)

Whitehead
Mohoua albicilla
To 15 cm (6 in.)

Grey Warbler
Gerygone igata
To 10 cm (4 in.)
Note red eye.

Song Thrush
Turdus philomelos
To 23 cm (9 in.)
Named for its rich,
loud, clear song which
is a series of repeated
phrases separated by
brief pauses.

Saddleback
Philesturnus carunculatus
To 25 cm (10 in.)
Note red wattles
at base of bill.

Tomtit
Petroica macrocephala
To 13 cm (5 in.)

Fantail
Rhipidura fuliginosa To 15 cm (6 in.)
Subspecies range in color from grey-
brown to black. Active and restless,
it fans its tail when perching. One
of New Zealand's most familiar and
widespread species.

Dollarbird
Eurystomus orientalis
To 30 cm (12 in.)
Named for pale, coin-
shaped patches on
its wingtips that are
evident in flight.

New Zealand Pipit
Anthus novaeseelandiae
To 20 cm (8 in.)
More slender than
the similar skylark, it
constantly flicks its tail
while foraging.

Brown Creeper
Mohoua novaeseelandiae
To 13 cm (5 in.)
Creeps around tree trunks
and branches – often
upside-down – while
foraging for insects.

Silvereye
Zosterops lateralis
To 13 cm (5 in.)
Note prominent
white eye ring.

Dunnock (Hedge Sparrow)
Prunella modularis
To 15 cm (6 in.)
Note grey on head
and breast.

Starling
Sturnus vulgaris
To 20 cm (8 in.)

Common Myna
Acridotheres tristis
To 23 cm (9 in.)

Blackbird
Turdus merula
To 25 cm (10 in.)
Females are brownish.

Masked Woodswallow
Artamus personatus
To 20 cm (8 in.)

Rook
Corvus frugilegus
To 45 cm (18 in.)
Note pale grey skin
at base of beak.

Red-vented Bulbul
Pycnonotus cafer
To 23 cm (9 in.)
Popular cage bird
was introduced
from Asia.

Australian Magpie
Gymnorhina tibicen
To 40 cm (16 in.)

Kokako
Callaeas cinerea
To 40 cm (16 in.)
Note blue wattles
at base of bill. More
often seen than heard,
its extraordinary,
complex, flute-like
songs are most often
heard at dawn.

Black-faced Cuckoo-shrike
Coracina novaehollandiae
To 35 cm (14 in.)

Fernbird
Bowdleria punctata
To 18 cm (7 in.)
Secretive bird can be
found skulking around
in dense vegetation.
Long tail is ragged.

Cirl Bunting
Emberiza cirlus
To 15 cm (6 in.)

New Zealand Robin
Petroica australis
To 18 cm (7 in.)
Drab, greyish bird
has long legs.

Chaffinch
Fringilla coelebs
To 15 cm (6 in.)
Note white shoulders.

Bellbird
Anthornis melanura
To 20 cm (8 in.)
Widespread and
abundant. One of its
songs is a series of
clear, bell-like notes.

Stitchbird
Notiomystis cincta
To 20 cm (8 in.)

Yellowhammer
Emberiza citrinella
To 15 cm (6 in.)

Greenfinch
Chloris chloris
To 15 cm (6 in.)
Female is similar
but paler green.

Tui
Prosthemadera novaeseelandiae
To 30 cm (12 in.)
Plumage is metallic
green, blue and
copper. Note white
throat plumes.

Redpoll
Acanthis flammea
To 13 cm (5 in.)

House Sparrow
Passer domesticus
To 15 cm (6 in.)

Goldfinch
Carduelis carduelis
To 13 cm (5 in.)